Pope Leo XIII

Immoratie Dei

encyclical letter of Our Holy Father - Pope Leo XIII on the christian

constitution of states

Pope Leo XIII

Immoratie Dei
encyclical letter of Our Holy Father - Pope Leo XIII on the christian constitution of states

ISBN/EAN: 9783337089948

Printed in Europe, USA, Canada, Australia, Japan

Cover: Foto ©Lupo / pixelio.de

More available books at **www.hansebooks.com**

ENCYCLICAL LETTER

OF

OUR HOLY FATHER

BY DIVINE PROVIDENCE

POPE LEO THE THIRTEENTH

ON THE

CHRISTIAN CONSTITUTION

OF STATES.

———

Latin Text and Authorised Translation.

———

LONDON.

1886.

LEO PP. XIII.

VENERABILES FRATRES

SALUTEM ET APOSTOLICAM BENEDICTIONEM.

IMMORTALE Dei miserentis opus, quod est Ecclesia, quamquam per se et natura sua salutem spectat animorum adipiscendamque in caelis felicitatem, tamen in ipso etiam rerum mortalium genere tot ac tantas ultro parit utilitates, ut plures maioresve non posset, si in primis et maxime esset ad tuendam huius vitae, quae in terris agitur, prosperitatem institutum.—Revera quacumque Ecclesia vestigium posuit, continuo rerum faciem immutavit, popularesque mores sicut virtutibus antea ignotis, ita et nova urbanitate imbuit: quam quotquot accepere populi, mansuetudine, aequitate, rerum gestarum gloria excelluerunt.—Sed vetus tamen illa est atque antiqua vituperatio, quod Ecclesiam aiunt esse cum rationibus reipublicae dissidentem, nec quicquam posse ad ea vel commoda vel ornamenta conferre, quae suo iure suaque sponte omnis bene constituta civitas appetit. Sub ipsis Ecclesiae primordiis non dissimili opinionis iniquitate agitari christianos, et in odium invidiamque vocari solitos hac etiam de caussa accepimus, quod hostes imperii dicerentur: quo tempore malorum culpam, quibus esset perculsa respublica, vulgo libebat in christianum conferre nomen, cum revera ultor scelorum Deus poenas a sontibus iustas exigeret. Eius atrocitas calumniae non sine caussa ingenium armavit stilumque acuit Augustini: qui praesertim in *Civitate Dei* virtutem christianae sapientiae, qua parte necessitudinem habet cum re publica, tanto in lumine collocavit, ut non tam pro christianis sui temporis dixisse caussam, quam de criminibus falsis perpetuum triumphum egisse videatur.—Similium tamen querelarum atque insimulationum funesta libido non quievit, ac permultis sane placuit civilem vivendi disciplinam aliunde petere, quam ex doctrinis, quas Ecclesia catholica probat. Immo postremo hoc tempore *novum*, ut appellant, *ius*, quod inquiunt esse velut quoddam adulti iam saeculi incrementum, progrediente libertate partum, valere ac dominari passim coepit.— Sed quantumvis multa multi periclitati sunt, constat, repertam numquam esse praestantiorem constituendae temperandaeque civitatis rationem, quam quae ab evangelica doctrina sponte efflorescit. — Maximi igitur momenti atque admodum muneri Nostro apostolico consentaneum esse arbitramur, novas de re publica opiniones cum doctrina christiana conferre : quo modo erroris dubitationisque caussas ereptum iri, emergente veritate, confidimus, ita ut videre quisque facile queat summa illa praecepta vivendi, quae sequi et quibus parere debeat.

Non est magni negotii statuere, qualem sit speciem formamque habitura civitas, gubernante christiana philosophia rem publicam.— Insitum homini natura est, ut in civili societate vivat : is enim necessarium vitae cultum et paratum, itemque ingenii atque animi perfectionem cum in solitudine adipisci non possit, provisum divinitus est, ut ad coniunctionem congregationemque hominum nasceretur cum domesticam, tum etiam civilem, quae suppeditare *vitae sufficientiam perfectam* sola potest. Quoniam vero non potest societas ulla consistere, nisi si aliquis omnibus praesit, efficaci similique movens singulos ad commune propositum impulsione, efficitur, civili hominum communitati necessariam esse auctoritatem, qua regatur : quae, non secus ac societas, a natura proptereaque a Deo ipso oriatur auctore.—Ex quo illud consequitur, potestatem publicam per se ipsam non esse nisi a Deo. Solus enim Deus est verissimus maximusque rerum dominus, cui subesse et servire omnia, quaecumque sunt, necesse est : ita ut quicumque ius imperandi habent, non id aliunde accipiant, nisi ab illo summo omnium principe Deo. *Non est potestas nisi a Deo.*[1]— Ius autem imperii per se non est cum ulla reipublicae forma necessario copulatum : aliam sibi vel aliam assumere recte potest, modo utilitatis bonique communis reapse efficientem. Sed in quolibet genere reipublicae omnino principes debent summum mundi gubernatorem Deum intueri, eumque sibimetipsis in ad-

[1] Rom. xiii. 1.

ministranda civitate tamquam exemplum legemque proponere.
Deus enim, sicut in rebus, quae sunt quaeque cernuntur, caussas genuit secundarias, in quibus perspici aliqua ratione posset
natura actioque divina, quaeque ad eum finem, quo haec rerum
spectat universitas, conducerent : ita in societate civili voluit esse
principatum, quem qui gererent, ii imaginem quamdam divinae
in genus humanum potestatis divinaeque providentiae referrent.
Debet igitur imperium iustum esse, neque herile, sed quasi pater-
num, quia Dei iustissima in homines potestas est et cum paterna
bonitate coniuncta : gerendum vero est ad utilitatem civium, quia
qui praesunt ceteris, hac una de caussa praesunt, ut civitatis
utilitatem tueantur. Neque ullo pacto committendum, unius ut,
vel paucorum commodo serviat civilis auctoritas, cum ad commune
omnium bonum constituta sit. Quod si, qui praesunt, delabantur
in dominatum iniustum, si importunitate superbiave peccaverint,
si male populo consuluerint, sciant sibi rationem aliquando Deo
esse reddendam, idque tanto severius, quanto vel sanctiore in
munere versati sint, vel gradum dignitatis altiorem obtinuerint.
Potentes potenter tormenta patientur.[1]—Ita sane maiestatem imperii
reverentia civium honesta et libens comitabitur. Etenim cum
semel in animum induxerint, pollere, qui imperant, auctoritate a
Deo data, illa quidem officia iusta ac debita esse sentient, dicto
audientes esse principibus, eisdemque obsequium ac fidem prae-
stare cum quadam similitudine pietatis, quae liberorum est erga
parentes. *Omnis anima potestatibus sublimioribus subdita sit.*[2]—
Spernere quippe potestatem legitimam, quavis eam in persona
esse constiterit, non magis licet, quam divinae voluntati resistere :
cui si qui resistant, in interitum ruunt voluntarium. *Qui resistit
potestati, Dei ordinationi resistit; qui autem resistunt, ipsi sibi damna-
tionem acquirunt.*[3] Quapropter obedientiam abiicere, et, per vim
multitudinis, rem ad seditionem vocare est crimen maiestatis,
neque humanae tantum, sed etiam divinae.

Hac ratione constitutam civitatem, perspicuum est, omnino
debere plurimis maximisque officiis, quae ipsam iungunt Deo, religione publica satisfacere.—Natura et ratio, quae iubet singulos
sancte religioseque Deum colere, quod in eius potestate sumus, et
quod ab eo profecti ad eumdem reverti debemus, eadem lege
adstringit civilem communitatem. Homines enim communi societate coniuncti nihilo sunt minus in Dei potestate, quam singuli :

---

[1] Sap. vi. 7.　　　[2] Rom. xiii. 1.　　　[3] Ibid. xiii. 2.

neque minorem, quam singuli, gratiam Deo societas debet, quo
auctore coaluit, cuius nutu conservatur, cuius beneficio innumera-
bilem bonorum, quibus affluit, copiam accepit. Quapropter sicut
nemini licet sua adversus Deum officia negligere, officiumque est
maximum amplecti et animo et moribus religionem, nec quam
quisque maluerit, sed quam Deus iusserit, quamque certis mini-
meque dubitandis indiciis unam ex omnibus veram esse constiterit: eodem modo civitates non possunt, citra scelus, gerere se
tamquam si Deus omnino non esset, aut curam religionis velut
alienam nihilque profuturam abiicere, aut asciscere de pluribus
generibus indifferenter quod libeat: omninoque debent eum in
colendo numine morem usurpare modumque, quo coli se Deus
ipse demonstravit velle.—Sanctum igitur oportet apud principes
esse Dei nomen; ponendumque in praecipuis illorum officiis religionem gratia complecti, benevolentia tueri, auctoritate nutuque
legum tegere, nec quippiam instituere aut decernere, quod sit eius
incolumitati contrarium. Id et civibus debent, quibus praesunt.
Nati enim susceptique omnes homines sumus ad summum quoddam
et ultimum bonorum, quo sunt omnia consilia referenda extra hanc
fragilitatem brevitatemque vitae in caelis collocatum. Quoniam
autem hinc pendet hominum undique expleta ac perfecta felicitas,
idcirco assequi eum, qui commemoratus est, finem tanti interest
singulorum, ut pluris interesse non possit. Civilem igitur societatem, communi utilitati natam, in tuenda prosperitate reipublicae
necesse est sic consulere civibus, ut obtinendo adipiscendoque
summo illi atque incommutabili bono quod sponte appetunt, non
modo nihil importet unquam incommodi, sed omnes quascumque
possit, opportunitates afferat. Quarum praecipua est, ut detur
opera religioni sancte inviolateque servandae, cuius officia hominem Deo coniungunt.

Vera autem religio quae sit, non difficulter videt qui iudicium
prudens sincerumque adhibuerit: argumentis enim permultis atque
illustribus, veritate nimirum vaticiniorum, prodigiorum frequentia,
celerrima fidei vel per medios hostes ac maxima impedimenta pro-
pagatione, martyrum testimonio, aliisque similibus liquet, eam
esse unice veram, quam Iesus Christus et instituit ipsemet et
Ecclesiae suae tuendam propagandamque demandavit.

Nam unigenitus Dei filius societatem in terris constituit, quae
Ecclesia dicitur, cui excelsum divinumque munus in omnes saecu-
lorum aetates continuandum transmisit, quod Ipse a Patre acce-

perat. *Sicut misit me Pater, et ego mitto vos.*[1]—*Ecce ego vobiscum
sum omnibus diebus usque ad consummationem saeculi.*[2] Igitur sicut
Iesus Christus in terras venit ut homines *vitam habeant et abun-
dantius habeant,*[3] eodem modo Ecclesia propositum habet, tamquam
finem, salutem animorum sempiternam: ob eamque rem talis est
natura sua, ut porrigat sese ad totius complexum gentis humanae,
nullis nec locorum nec temporum limitibus circumscripta. *Prae-
dicate Evangelium omni creaturae.*[4]—Tam ingenti hominum multi-
tudini Deus ipse magistratus assignavit, qui cum potestate
praeessent: unumque omnium principem, et maximum certissi-
mumque veritatis magistrum esse voluit, cui claves regni caelorum
commisit. *Tibi dabo claves regni caelorum.*[5]—*Pasce agnos . . . .
pasce oves:*[6] *ego rogavi pro te, ut non deficiat fides tua.*[7]—Haec
societas, quamvis ex hominibus constet, non secus ac civilis com-
munitas, tamen propter finem sibi constitutum, atque instru-
menta, quibus ad finem contendit, supernaturalis est et spiritualis:
atque idcirco distinguitur ac differt a societate civili: et, quod
plurimum interest, societas est genere et iure perfecta, cum
adiumenta ad incolumitatem actionemque suam necessaria, voluntate beneficioque conditoris sui, omnia in se et per se ipsa
possideat. Sicut finis, quo tendit Ecclesia, longe nobilissimus
est, ita eius potestas est omnium praestantissima, neque imperio civili potest haberi inferior, aut eidem esse ullo modo
obnoxia.—Revera Iesus Christus Apostolis suis libera mandata
dedit in sacra, adiuncta tum ferendarum legum veri nominis
facultate, tum gemina, quae hinc consequitur, iudicandi punien-
dique potestate. "*Data est mihi omnis potestas in caelo et in
terra: euntes ergo docete omnes gentes . . . . docentes eos servare
omnia quaecumque mandavi vobis.*"[8] Et alibi: "*Si non audierit eos,
dic Ecclesiae.*"[9] Atque iterum: "*In promptu habentes ulcisci omnem
inobedientiam.*"[10] Rursus: "*durius agam secundum potestatem, quam
Dominus dedit mihi in aedificationem et non in destructionem.*"[11] Itaque
dux hominibus esse ad caelestia, non civitas sed Ecclesia debet:
eidemque hoc est munus assignatum a Deo, ut de iis, quae religionem attingunt, videat ipsa et statuat: ut doceat omnes
gentes: ut christiani nominis fines, quoad potest, late proferat:
brevi, ut rem christianam libere expediteque iudicio suo adminis-

---

[1] Ioan. xx. 21. [2] Matt. xxviii. 20. [3] Ioan. x. 10. [4] Marc. xvi. 15.
[5] Matt. xvi. 19. [6] Ioan. xxi. 16, 17. [7] Luc. xxii. 32.
[8] Matt. xxviii, 18, 19, 20. [9] Ibid. xviii. 17. [10] 2 Cor. x. 6. [11] Ibid. xiii. 10.

8

tret.—Hanc vero auctoritatem in se ipsa absolutam planeque sui
iuris, quae ab assentatrice principum philosophia iamdiu oppug-
natur, Ecclesia sibi asserere itemque publice exercere numquam
desiit, primis omnium pro ea propugnantibus Apostolis, qui cum
disseminare Evangelium a principibus Synagogae prohiberentur,
constanter respondebant, *obedire oportet Deo magis, quam hominibus*.[1]
Eamdem sancti Ecclesiae Patres rationum momentis tueri pro
opportunitate studuerunt: romanique Pontifices invicta animi
constantia adversus oppugnatores vindicare numquam praetermi-
serunt.—Quin etiam et opinione et re eamdem probarunt ipsi viri
principes rerumque publicarum gubernatores, ut qui paciscendo,
transigendis negotiis, mittendis vicissimque accipiendis legatis,
atque aliorum mutatione officiorum, agere cum Ecclesia tamquam
cum suprema potestate legitima consueverunt.—Neque profecto
sine singulari providentis Dei consilio factum esse censendum est,
ut haec ipsa potestas principatu civili, velut optima libertatis suae
tutela, muniretur.

Itaque Deus humani generis procurationem inter duas potes-
tates partitus est, scilicet ecclesiasticam et civilem, alteram quidem
divinis, alteram humanis rebus praepositam. Utraque est in suo
genere maxima: habet utraque certos, quibus contineatur, ter-
minos, eosque sua cuiusque natura caussaque proxima definitos;
unde aliquis velut orbis circumscribitur, in quo sua cuiusque actio
iure proprio versetur. Sed quia utriusque imperium est in eosdem,
cum usuvenire possit, ut res una atque eadem, quamquam aliter
atque aliter, sed tamen eadem res ad utriusque ius iudiciumque
pertineat, debet providentissimus Deus, a quo sunt ambae constitutae,
utriusque itinera recte atque ordine composuisse. *Quae autem sunt
a Deo ordinatae sunt.*[2] Quod ni ita esset, funestarum saepe conten-
tionum concertationumque caussae nascerentur; nec raro sollicitus
animi, velut in via ancipiti, haerere homo deberet, anxius quid
facto opus esset, contraria iubentibus binis potestatibus, quarum
recusare imperium, salvo officio, non potest. Atqui maxime istud
repugnat de sapientia cogitare et bonitate Dei, qui vel in rebus
phisicis, quamquam sunt longe inferioris ordinis, tamen naturales
vires caussasque invicem conciliavit moderata ratione et quodam
velut concentu mirabili, ita ut nulla earum impediat ceteras,
cunctaeque simul illuc, quo mundus spectat, convenienter aptissi-
meque conspirent.—Itaque inter utramque potestatem quaedam

1 Act. v. 29.   [2] Rom. xiii. 1.

intercedat necesse est ordinata colligatio : quae quidem coniunctioni non immerito comparatur, per quam anima et corpus in homine copulantur. Qualis autem et quanta ea sit, aliter iudicari non potest, nisi respiciendo, uti diximus, ad utriusque naturam, habendàque ratione excellentiae et nobilitatis caussarum; cum alteri proxime maximeque propositum sit rerum mortalium curare commoda, alteri caelestia ac sempiterna bona comparare.—Quidquid igitur est in rebus humanis quoquo modo sacrum, quidquid ad salutem animorum cultumve Dei pertinet, sive tale illud sit natura sua, sive rursus tale intelligatur propter caussam ad quam refertur, id est omne in potestate arbitrioque Ecclesiae : cetera vero, quae civile et politicum genus complectitur, rectum est civili auctoritati esse subiecta, cum Iesus Christus iusserit, quae Caesaris sint, reddi Caesari, quae Dei, Deo.—Incidunt autem quandoque tempora, cum alius quoque concordiae modus ad tranquillam libertatem valet, nimirum si qui principes rerum publicarum et Pontifex romanus de re aliqua separata in idem placitum consenserint. Quibus Ecclesia temporibus maternae pietatis eximia documenta praebet, cum facilitatis indulgentiaeque tantum adhibere soleat, quantum maxime potest.

Eiusmodi est, quam summatim attigimus, civilis hominum societatis christiana temperatio, et haec non temere neque ad libidinem ficta, sed ex maximis ducta verissimisque principiis, quae ipsa naturali ratione confirmantur.

Talis autem conformatio reipublicae nihil habet, quod poss aut minus videri dignum amplitudine principum, aut parum decorum : tantumque abest, ut iura maiestatis imminuat, ut potius stabiliora atque augustiora faciat. Immo, si altius consideretur, habet illa conformatio perfectionem quamdam magnam, qua carent ceteri rerum publicarum modi : ex eâque fructus essent sane excellentes et varii consecuturi, si modo suum partes singulae gradum tenerent, atque illud integre efficerent, cui unaquaeque praeposita est, officium et munus.—Revera in ea, quam ante diximus, constitutione reipublicae, sunt quidem divina atque humana convenienti ordine partita : incolumia civium iura, eademque divinarum, naturalium, humanarumque legum patrocinio defensa : officiorum singulorum cum sapienter constituta descriptio, tum opportune sancita custodia. Singuli homines in hoc ad sempiternam illam civitatem dubio laboriosoque curriculo sibi sciunt praesto esse, quos tuto sequantur ad ingrediendum duces,

ad perveniendum adiutores: pariterque intelligunt, sibi alios
esse ad securitatem, ad fortunas, ad commoda cetera, quibus
communis haec vita constat, vel parienda vel conservanda
datos.—Societas domestica eam, quam par est, firmitudinem
adipiscitur ex unius atque individui sanctitate coniugii: iura
officiaque inter coniuges sapienti iustitia et aequitate re-
guntur: debitum conservatur mulieri decus: auctoritas viri ad
exemplum est auctoritatis Dei conformata: temperata patria
potestas convenienter dignitati uxoris prolisque: denique liberorum tuitioni, commodis, institutioni optime consulitur.—In
genere rerum politico et civili, leges spectant commune bonum,
neque voluntate iudicioque fallaci multitudinis, sed veritate iusti-
tiaque diriguntur: auctoritas principum sanctitudinem quamdam
induit humana maiorem, contineturque ne declinet a iustitia, neu
modum in imperando transiliat: obedientia civium habet honestatem dignitatemque comitem, quia non est hominis ad hominem
servitus, sed obtemperatio voluntati Dei, regnum per homines
exercentis. Quo cognito ac persuaso, omnino ad iustitiam pertinere illa intelliguntur, vereri maiestatem principum, subesse
constanter et fideliter potestati publicae, nihil seditiose facere,
sanctam servare disciplinam civitatis.—Similiter ponitur in officiis
caritas mutua, benignitas, liberalitas: non distrahitur in contrarias partes, pugnantibus inter se praeceptis, civis idem et chris-
tianus: denique amplissima bona, quibus mortalem quoque hominum vitam christiana religio sua sponte explet, communitati
societatique civili omnia quaeruntur: ita ut illud appareat veris-
sime dictum, "pendet a religione, qua Deus colitur, rei publicae
status: multaque inter hunc et illam cognatio et familiaritas
intercedit."[1]—Eorum vim bonorum mirabiliter, uti solet, perse-
cutus est Augustinus pluribus locis, maxime vero ubi Ecclesiam
catholicam appellat iis verbis: "Tu pueriliter pueros, fortiter
iuvenes, quiete senes, prout cuiusque non corporis tantum, sed et
animi aetas est, exerces ac doces. Tu feminas viris suis non ad
explendam libidinem, sed ad propagandam prolem, et ad rei
familiaris societatem, casta et fideli obedientia subiicis. Tu viros
coniugibus, non ad illudendum imbecilliorem sexum, sed sinceri
amoris legibus praeficis. Tu parentibus filios libera quadam
servitute subiungis, parentes filiis pia dominatione praeponis. . . .

---

[1] Sacr. Imp. ad Cyrillum Alexand. et Episcopos metrop.—Cfr. Labbeum
Collect. Conc. t. iii.

Tu cives civibus, tu gentes gentibus, et prorsus homines primorum parentum recordatione, non societate tantum, sed quadam etiam fraternitate coniungis. Doces reges prospicere populis, mones populos se subdere regibus. Quibus honor debeatur, quibus affectus, quibus reverentia, quibus timor, quibus consolatio, quibus admonitio, quibus cohortatio, quibus disciplina, quibus obiurgatio, quibus supplicium, sedulo doces; ostendens quemadmodum et non omnibus omnia, et omnibus caritas, et nulli debeatur iniuria."[1]—Idemque alio loco male sapientes reprehendens politicos philosophos : " Qui doctrinam Christi adversam dicunt esse reipublicae, dent exercitum talem, quales doctrina Christi esse milites iussit, dent tales provinciales, tales maritos, tales coniuges, tales parentes, tales filios, tales dominos, tales servos, tales reges, tales iudices, tales denique debitorum ipsius fisci redditores et exactores, quales esse praecipit doctrina christiana, et audeant eam dicere adversam esse reipublicae, immo vero non dubitent eam confiteri magnam, si obtemperetur, salutem esse reipublicae."[2]

Fuit aliquando tempus, cum evangelica philosophia gubernaret civitates : quo tempore christianae sapientiae vis illa et divina virtus in leges, instituta, mores populorum, in omnes reipublicae ordines rationesque penetraverat : cum religio per Iesum Christum instituta in eo, quo aequum erat, dignitatis gradu firmiter collocata, gratia principum legitimâque magistratuum tutelâ ubique floreret: cum sacerdotium atque imperium concordia et amica officiorum vicissitudo auspicato coniungeret. Eoque modo composita civitas fructus tulit omni opinione maiores, quorum viget memoria et vigebit innumerabilibus rerum gestarum consignata monumentis, quae nulla adversariorum arte corrumpi aut obscurari possunt.—Quod Europa christiana barbaras gentes edomuit, easque a feritate ad mansuetudinem, a superstitione ad veritatem traduxit: quod Maomethanorum incursiones victrix propulsavit: quod civilis cultus principatum retinuit, et ad omne decus humanitatis ducem se magistramque praebere ceteris consuevit: quod germanam libertatem eamque multiplicem gratificata populis est : quod complura ad miseriarum solatium sapientissime instituit, sine controversia magnam debet gratiam

---

1 *De Moribus Eccl. Cath.*, cap. xxx. n. 63.
2 Epist. cxxxviii. (al. 5) ad Marcellinum, cap. ii. n. 15.

religioni, quam ad tantas res suscipiendas habuit auspicem, ad perficiendas adiutricem.—Mansissent profecto eadem bona, si utriusque potestatis concordia mansisset: maioraque expectari iure poterant, si auctoritati, si magisterio, si consiliis Ecclesiae maiore esset cum fide perseverantiaque obtemperatum. Illud enim perpetuae legis instar habendum est, quod Ivo Carnutensis ad Paschalem II. Pontificem maximum perscripsit, " cum regnum et sacerdotium inter se conveniunt, bene regitur mundus, floret et fructificat Ecclesia. Cum vero inter se discordant, non tantum parvae res non crescunt, sed etiam magnae res miserabiliter dilabuntur."[1]

Sed perniciosa illa ac deploranda rerum novarum studia, quae saeculo xvi. excitata sunt, cum primum religionem christianam miscuissent, mox naturali quodam itinere ad philosophiam, a philosophia ad omnes civilis communitatis ordines pervenerunt. Ex hoc velut fonte repetenda illa recentiora effrenatae libertatis capita, nimirum in maximis perturbationibus superiore saeculo excogitata in medioque proposita, perinde ac principia et fundamenta *novi iuris*, quod et fuit antea ignotum, et a iure non solum christiano, sed etiam naturali plus una ex parte discrepat.—Eorum principiorum illud est maximum, omnes homines, quemadmodum genere naturâque similes intelliguntur, ita reapse esse in actione vitae inter se pares: unumquemque ita esse sui iuris, ut nullo modo sit alterius auctoritati obnoxius: cogitare de re qualibet quae velit, agere quod lubeat, libere posse: imperandi aliis ius esse in nemine. His informata disciplinis societate, principatus non est nisi populi voluntas, qui, ut in sui ipsius unice est potestate, ita sibimetipsi solus imperat: deligit autem, quibus se committat, ita tamen ut imperii non tam ius, quam munus in eos transferat, idque suo nomine exercendum. In silentio iacet dominatio divina, non secus ac vel Deus aut nullus esset, aut humani generis societatem nihil curaret; vel homines sive singuli sive sociati nihil Deo deberent, vel principatus cogitari posset ullus, cuius non in Deo ipso caussa et vis et auctoritas tota resideat. Quo modo, ut perspicitur, est respublica nihil aliud nisi magistra et gubernatrix sui multitudo: cumque populus omnium iurium omnisque potestatis fontem in se ipse continere dicatur, consequens erit, ut nulla ratione officii obligatam Deo se civitas

[1] Ep. ccxxxviii.

putet; ut religionem publice profiteatur nullam; nec debeat ex pluribus quae vera sola sit, quaerere, nec unam quamdam ceteris anteponere, nec uni maxime favere, sed singulis generibus aequabilitatem iuris tribuere ad eum finem, dum disciplina reipublicae ne quid ab illis detrimenti capiat. Consentaneum erit, iudicio singulorum permittere omnem de religione quaestionem; licere cuique aut sequi quam ipse malit, aut omnino nullam, si nullam probet. Hinc profecto illa nascuntur; exlex uniuscuiusque conscientiae iudicium; liberrimae de Deo colendo, de non colendo, sententiae; infinita tum cogitandi, tum cogitata publicandi licentia.

Iis autem positis, quae maxime probantur hoc tempore, fundamentis reipublicae, facile apparet, quem in locum quamque iniquum compellatur Ecclesia.—Nam ubi cum eiusmodi doctrinis actio rerum consentiat, nomini catholico par cum societatibus ab eo alienis vel etiam inferior locus in civitate tribuitur: legum ecclesiasticarum nulla habetur ratio: Ecclesia, quae iussu mandatoque Iesu Christi docere omnes gentes debet, publicam populi institutionem iubetur nihil attingere.—De ipsis rebus, quae sunt mixti iuris, per se statuunt gubernatores rei civilis arbitratu suo, in eoque genere sanctissimas Ecclesiae leges superbe contemnunt. Quare ad iurisdictionem suam trahunt matrimonia christianorum, decernendo etiam de maritali vinculo, de unitate, de stabilitate coniugii: movent possessiones clericorum, quod res suas Ecclesiam tenere posse negant. Ad summam, sic agunt cum Ecclesia, ut societatis perfectae genere et iuribus opinione detractis, plane similem habeant ceterarum communitatum, quas respublica continet: ob eamque rem si quid illa iuris, si quid possidet facultatis ad agendum legitimae, possidere dicitur concessu beneficioque principum civitatis.—Si qua vero in republica suum Ecclesia ius, ipsis civilibus legibus probantibus, teneat, publiceque inter utramque potestatem pactio aliqua facta sit, principio clamant, dissociari Ecclesiae rationes a reipublicae rationibus oportere; idque eo consilio, ut facere contra interpositam fidem impune liceat, omniumque rerum habere, remotis impedimentis, arbitrium.—Id vero cum patienter ferre Ecclesia non possit, neque enim potest officia deserere sanctissima et maxima, omninoque postulet, ut obligata sibi fides integre religioseque solvatur, saepe sacram inter ac civilem potestatem dimicationes nascuntur, quarum ille ferme est exitus, alteram, ut quae minus est opibus humanis valida, alteri ut validiori succumbere.

Ita Ecclesiam, in hoc rerum publicarum statu, qui nunc a plerisque adamatur, mos et voluntas est, aut prorsus de medio pellere, aut vinctam adstrictamque imperio tenere. Quae publice aguntur, eo consilio magnam partem aguntur. Leges, administratio civitatum, expers religionis adolescentium institutio, spoliatio excidiumque ordinum religiosorum, eversio principatus civilis Pontificum romanorum, huc spectant omnia, incidere nervos institutorum christianorum, Ecclesiaeque catholicae et libertatem in angustum deducere, et iura cetera comminuere.

Eiusmodi de regenda civitate sententias ipsa naturalis ratio convincit, a veritate dissidere plurimum.—Quidquid enim potestatis usquam est, a Deo tamquam maximo augustissimoque fonte proficisci, ipsa natura testatur. Imperium autem populare, quod, nullo ad Deum respectu, in multitudine inesse natura dicitur, si praeclare ad suppeditandum valet blandimenta et flammas multarum cupiditatum, nulla quidem nititur ratione probabili, neque satis habere virium potest ad securitatem publicam quietamque ordinis constantiam. Revera his doctrinis res inclinavere usque eo, ut haec a pluribus tamquam lex in civili prudentia sanciatur, seditiones posse iure conflari. Valet enim opinio, nihilo principes pluris esse, quam delectos quosdam, qui voluntatem popularem exequantur : ex quo fit, quod necesse est, ut omnia sint pariter cum populi arbitrio mutabilia, et timor aliquis turbarum semper impendeat.

De religione autem putare, nihil inter formas dispares et contrarias interesse, hunc plane habet exitum, nolle ullam probare iudicio, nolle usu. Atqui istud ab atheismo, si nomine aliquid differt, re nihil differt. Quibus enim Deum esse persuasum est, ii, modo constare sibi nec esse perabsurdi velint, necessario intelligunt, usitatas in cultu divino rationes, quarum tanta est differentia maximisque etiam de rebus dissimilitudo et pugna, acque probabiles, aeque bonas, aeque Deo acceptas esse omnes non posse.

Sic illa quidlibet sentiendi litterarumque formis quidlibet exprimendi facultas, omni moderatione posthabita, non quoddam est propria vi sua bonum, quo societas humana iure laetetur : sed multorum malorum fons et origo.—Libertas, ut quae virtus est hominem perficiens, debet in eo quod verum sit, quodque bonum, versari : boni autem verique ratio mutari ad hominis arbitrium non potest, sed manet semper eadem, neque minus est, quam ipsa rerum natura, incommutabilis. Si mens adsentiatur opinionibus falsis, si malum voluntas adsumat et ad id se applicet, perfectionem sui neutra consequitur, sed excidunt dignitate naturali et in corruptelam ambae delabuntur. Quaecumque sunt igitur virtuti veritatique contraria, ea in luce atque in oculis hominum ponere non est aequum : gratia tutelâve legum defendere, multo minus. Sola bene acta vita via est in caelum, quo tendimus universi : ob eamque rem aberrat civitas a regula et praescriptione naturae, si licentiam opinionum praveque factorum in tantum lascivire sinat, ut impune liceat mentes a veritate, animos a virtute deducere.—Ecclesiam vero, quam Deus ipse constituit, ab actione vitae excludere, a legibus, ab institutione adolescentium, a societate domestica, magnus et perniciosus est error. Bene morata civitas esse, sublata religione, non potest : iamque plus fortasse, quam oporteret, est cognitum, qualis in se sit et quorsum pertineat illa de vita et moribus philosophia, quam *civilem* nominant. Vera est magistra virtutis et custos morum Ecclesia Christi : ea est, quae incolumia tuetur principia, unde officia ducuntur, propositisque caussis ad honeste vivendum efficacissimis, iubet non solum fugere prave facta, sed regere motus animi rationi contrarios etiam sine effectu.—Ecclesiam vero in suorum officiorum munere potestati civili velle esse subiectam, magna quidem iniuria, magna temeritas est. Hoc facto perturbatur ordo, quia quae naturalia sunt praeponuntur iis, quae sunt supra naturam : tollitur aut certe magnopere minuitur frequentia bonorum, quibus, si nulla re impediretur, communem vitam Ecclesia compleret : praetereaque via ad inimicitias munitur et certamina, quae quantam utrique reipublicae perniciem afferant, nimis saepe eventus demonstravit.

Huiusmodi doctrinas, quae nec humanae rationi probantur, et plurimum habent in civilem disciplinam momenti, romani Pontifices decessores Nostri, cum probe intelligerent quid a se postularet apostolicum munus, impune abire nequaquam passi sunt. Sic Gregorius XVI. per Encyclicas litteras hoc initio *Mirari vos* die xv. Augusti anno MDCCCXXXII., magna sententiarum gravitate ea perculit, quae iam praedicabantur, in cultu divino nullum adhibere delectum oportere : integrum singulis esse, quod malint, de religione iudicare : solam cuique suam esse conscientiam iudicem : praeterea edere quae quisque senserit, itemque res moliri novas in civitate licere. De rationibus rei sacrae reique civilis distrahendis sic idem Pontifex : "Neque laetiora et religioni et principatui ominari possemus ex eorum votis, qui Ecclesiam a regno separari, mutuamque imperii cum sacerdotio concordiam abrumpi discupiunt. Constat quippe, pertimesci ab impudentissimae libertatis amatoribus concordiam illam, quae semper rei et sacrae et civili fausta extitit et salutaris.''—Non absimili modo Pius IX., ut sese opportunitas dedit, ex opinionibus falsis, quae maxime valere coepissent, plures notavit, easdemque postea in unum cogi iussit, ut scilicet in tanta errorum colluvione haberent catholici homines, quod sine offensione sequerentur.[1]

Ex iis autem Pontificum praescriptis illa omnino intelligi necesse est, ortum publicae potestatis a Deo ipso, non a multitudine repeti oportere : seditionum licentiam cum ratione pugnare : officia religionis nullo loco numerare, vel uno modo esse in disparibus generibus affectos, nefas esse privatis hominibus, nefas civitatibus : immoderatam sentiendi sensusque palam iactandi potestatem non esse in civium iuribus neque in rebus gratia patrocinioque dignis ulla ratione ponendam.—Similiter intelligi debet, Ecclesiam societatem esse, non minus quam ipsam civitatem, genere et iure perfectam : neque debere, qui summam imperii teneant, committere ut sibi servire aut subesse Ecclesiam cogant, aut minus esse sinant ad suas res agendas liberam, aut quicquam de ceteris iuribus detrahant, quae in ipsam a Iesu Christo collata sunt.—In negotiis autem mixti iuris, maxime esse secundum naturam itemque secundum Dei consilia non secessionem alterius potestatis ab altera, multoque minus contentionem, sed plane concordiam, eamque cum caussis proximis congruentem, quae caussae utramque societatem genuerunt.

Haec quidem sunt, quae de constituendis temperandisque civitatibus ab Ecclesia catholica praecipiuntur.—Quibus tamen dictis decretisque si recte diiudicari velit, nulla per se reprehenditur ex variis reipublicae formis, ut quae nihil habent, quod

---

[1] Earum nonnullas indicare sufficiat :
Prop. xix. Ecclesia non est vera perfectaque societas plane libera, nec pollet suis propriis et constantibus iuribus sibi a divino suo Fundatore collatis, sed civilis potestatis est definire quae sint Ecclesiae iura ac limites, intra quos eadem iura exercere queat.
Prop. xxxix. Reipublicae status, upote omnium iurium origo et fons, iure quodam pollet nullis circumscripto limitibus.
Prop. lv. Ecclesia a Statu, Statusque ab Ecclesia seiungendus est.
Prop. lxxix. . . . falsum est, civilem cuiusque cultus libertatem, itemque plenam potestatem omnibus attributam quaslibet opiniones cogitationesque palam publiceque manifestandi, conducere ad populorum mores animosque facilius corrumpendos, ao indifferentismi pestem propagandam.

doctrinae catholicae repugnet, eaedemque possunt, si sapienter adhibeantur et iuste, in optimo statu tueri civitatem.—Immo neque illud per se reprehenditur, participem plus minus esse populum rei publicae: quod ipsum certis in temporibus certisque legibus potest non solum ad utilitatem, sed etiam ad officium pertinere civium.—Insuper neque caussa iusta nascitur, cur Ecclesiam quisquam criminetur, aut esse in lenitate facilitateque plus aequo restrictam, aut ei, quae germana et legitima sit, libertati inimicam.—Revera si divini cultus varia genera eodem iure esse, quo veram religionem, Ecclesia iudicat non licere, non ideo tamen eos damnat rerum publicarum moderatores, qui, magni alicuius aut adipiscendi boni, aut prohibendi caussa mali, moribus atque usu patienter ferunt, ut ea habeant singula in civitate locum.—Atque illud quoque magnopere cavere Ecclesia solet ut ad amplexandam fidem catholicam nemo invitus cogatur, quia, quod sapienter Augustinus monet, *credere non potest homo nisi volens.*[1]

Simili ratione nec potest Ecclesia libertatem probare eam, quae fastidium gignat sanctissimarum Dei legum, debitamque potestati legitimae obedientiam exuat. Est enim licentia verius, quam libertas; rectissimeque ab Augustino *libertas perditionis,*[2] a Petro Apostolo *velamen malitiae*[3] appellatur: immo, cum sit praeter rationem, vera servitus est: *qui,* enim, *facit peccatum, servus est peccati.*[4] Contra illa germana est atque expetenda libertas, quae si privatim spectetur, erroribus et cupiditatibus, teterrimis dominis, hominem servire non sinit: si publice, civibus sapienter praeest, facultatem augendorum commodorum large ministrat: remque publicam ab alieno arbitrio defendit.—Atqui honestam hanc et homine dignam libertatem, Ecclesia probat omnium maxime, eamque ut tueretur in populis firmam atque integram, eniti et contendere numquam destitit.—Revera quae res in civitate plurimum ad communem salutem possunt: quae sunt contra licentiam principum populo male consulentium utiliter institutae; quae summam rempublicam vetant in municipalem, vel domesticam rem importunius invadere: quae valent ad decus, ad personam hominis, ad aequabilitatem iuris in singulis civibus conservandam, earum rerum omnium Ecclesiam catholicam vel inventricem, vel auspicem, vel custodem semper fuisse, superiorum aetatum monumenta testantur. Sibi igitur perpetuo con-

[1] Tract. xxvi. in Ioan. n. 2. [2] Epist. cv. ad Donatistas, cap. ii. n. 9.
[3] 1 Pet. ii. 16. [4] Ioan. viii. 34.

A 3

sentiens, si ex altera parte libertatem respuit immodicam, quae
et privatis et populis in licentiam vel in servitutem cadit, ex
altera volens et libens amplectitur res meliores, quas dies afferat,
si vero prosperitatem contineant huius vitae, quae quoddam est
velut stadium ad alteram eamque perpetuo mansuram.—Ergo
quod inquiunt, Ecclesiam recentiori civitatum invidere disciplinae,
et quaecumque horum temporum ingenium peperit, omnia pro-
miscue repudiare, inanis est et ieiuna calumnia. Insaniam
quidem repudiat opinionum : improbat nefaria seditionum studia,
illumque nominatim habitum animorum, in quo initia perspiciun-
tur voluntarii discessus a Deo : sed quia omne, quod verum est,
a Deo proficisci necesse est, quidquid, indagando, veri attinga-
tur, agnoscit Ecclesia velut quoddam divinae mentis vestigium.
Cumque nihil sit in rerum natura veri, quod doctrinis divinitus
traditis fidem abroget, multa quae adrogent, omnisque possit
inventio veri ad Deum ipsum vel cognoscendum vel laudandum
impellere, idcirco quidquid accedat ad scientiarum fines profer-
endos, gaudente et libente Ecclesia semper accedet : eademque
studiose, ut solet, sicut alias disciplinas, ita illas etiam fovebit ac
provehet, quae positae sunt in explicatione naturae. Quibus in
studiis, non adversatur Ecclesia si quid mens repererit novi : non
repugnat quin plura quaerantur ad decus commoditatemque vitae :
immo inertiae desidiaeque inimica, magnopere vult ut hominum
ingenia uberes ferant exercitatione et cultura fructus : incitamenta
praebet ad omne genus artium atque operum : omniaque harum
rerum studia ad honestatem salutemque virtute sua dirigens,
impedire nititur, quominus a Deo bonisque caelestibus sua hominem intelligentia atque industria deflectat.

Sed haec, tametsi plena rationis et consilii, minus probantur
hoc tempore, cum civitates non modo recusant sese ad christianae
sapientiae referre formam, sed etiam videntur quotidie longius ab
ea velle discedere.—Nihilominus quia in lucem prolata veritas solet
sua sponte late fluere, hominumque mentes sensim pervadere,
idcirco Nos conscientia maximi sanctissimique officii, hoc est
Apostolica, qua fungimur ad gentes universas, legatione permoti,
ea quae vera sunt, libere, ut debemus, eloquimur : non quod non
perspectam habeamus rationem temporum, aut repudianda aetatis
nostrae honesta atque utilia incrementa putemus, sed quod rerum
publicarum tutiora ab offensionibus itinera ac firmiora fundamenta
vellemus : idque incolumi populorum germana libertate ; in ho-

minibus enim mater et custos optima libertatis veritas est: *veritas liberabit vos.*[1]

Itaque in tam difficili rerum cursu, catholici homines, si Nos, ut oportet, audierint, facile videbunt quae sua cuiusque sint tam in *opinionibus,* quam in *factis* officia.—Et in opinando quidem, quaecumque Pontifices romani tradiderint vel tradituri sunt, singula necesse est et tenere iudicio stabili comprehensa, et palam, quoties res postulaverit, profiteri. Ac nominatim de iis, quas *libertates* vocant novissimo tempore quaesitas, oportet Apostolicae Sedis stare iudicio, et quod ipsa senserit, idem sentire singulos. Cavendum, ne quem fallat honesta illarum species: cogitandumque quibus ortae initiis, et quibus passim sustententur atque alantur studiis. Satis iam est experiendo cognitum, quarum illae rerum effectrices sint in civitate: eos quippe passim genuere fructus, quorum probos viros et sapientes iure poeniteat.—Si talis alicubi aut reapse sit, aut fingatur cogitatione civitas, quae christianum nomen insectetur proterve et tyrannice, cum eaque conferatur genus id reipublicae recens, de quo loquimur, poterit hoc videri tolerabilius. Principia tamen, quibus nititur, sunt profecto ciusmodi, sicut ante diximus, ut per se ipsa probari nemini debeant.

Potest tamen aut in privatis domesticisque rebus, aut in publicis actio versari.—Privatim quidem primum officium est, praeceptis evangelicis diligentissime conformare vitam et mores, nec recusare si quid christiana virtus exigat ad patiendum tolerandumque paulo difficilius. Debent praeterea singuli Ecclesiam sic diligere, ut communem matrem: eiusque et servare obedienter leges, et honori servire, et iura salva velle: conarique, ut ab iis, in quos quisque aliquid auctoritate potest, pari pietate colatur atque ametur.—Illud etiam publicae salutis interest, ad rerum urbanarum administrationem conferre sapienter operam: in eaque studere maxime et efficere, ut adolescentibus ad religionem, ad probos mores informandis ea ratione, qua aequum est christianis, publice consultum sit: quibus ex rebus magnopere pendet singularum salus civitatum.—Item catholicorum hominum operam ex hoc tamquam angustiore campo longius excurrere, ipsamque summam rempublicam complecti, generatim utile est atque honestum. *Generatim* eo dicimus, quia haec praecepta Nostra gentes univer-

[1] Ioan. viii. 32.

sas attingunt. Ceterum potest alicubi accidere, ut, maximis iustissimisque de caussis, rempublicam capessere, in muneribusque politicis versari, nequaquam expediat. Sed generatim, ut diximus, nullam velle rerum publicarum partem attingere tam esset in vitio, quam nihil ad communem utilitatem afferre studii, nihil operae: eo vel magis quod catholici homines ipsius, quam profitentur, admonitione doctrinae, ad rem integre et ex fide gerendam impelluntur. Contra, ipsis otiosis, facile habenas accepturi sunt ii, quorum opiniones spem salutis haud sane magnam afferant. Idque esset etiam cum pernicie coniunctum christiani nominis : propterea quod plurimum possent qui male essent in Ecclesiam animati; minimum, qui bene. Quamobrem perspicuum est, ad rempublicam adeundi caussam esse iustam catholicis : non enim adeunt, neque adire debent ob eam caussam, ut probent quod est hoc tempore in rerum publicarum rationibus non honestum ; sed ut has ipsas rationes, quoad fieri potest, in bonum publicum transferant sincerum atque verum, destinatum animo habentes, sapientiam virtutemque catholicae religionis, tamquam saluberrimum succum ac sanguinem, in omnes reipublicae venas inducere.—Haud aliter actum in primis Ecclesiae aetatibus. Mores enim et studia ethnicorum quam longissime a studiis abhorrebant moribusque evangelicis : christianos tamen cernere erat in media superstitione incorruptos semperque sui similes animose, quacumque daretur aditus, inferre sese. Fideles in exemplum principibus, obedientesque, quoad fas esset, imperio legum, fundebant mirificum splendorem sanctitatis usquequaque ; prodesse studebant fratribus, vocare ceteros ad sapientiam Christi, cedere tamen loco atque emori fortiter parati, si honores, si magistratus, si imperia retinere, incolumi virtute, nequivissent. Qua ratione celeriter instituta christiana non modo in privatas domos, sed in castra, in curiam, in ipsam regiam invexere. "Hesterni sumus, et vestra omnia implevimus, urbes, insulas, castella, municipia, conciliabula, castra ipsa, tribus, decurias, palatium, senatum, forum :"[1] ita ut fides christiana, cum Evangelium publice profiteri lege licuit, non in cunis vagiens, sed adulta et iam satis firma in magna civitatum parte apparuerit.

Iamvero his temporibus consentaneum est, haec maiorum exempla renovari.—Catholicos quidem, quotquot digni sunt eo nomine, primum omnium necesse est amantissimos Ecclesiae

[1] Tertull. Apol. n. 37.

filios et esse et videri velle : quae res nequeant cum hac laude
consistere, eas sine cunctatione respuere : institutis populorum,
quantum honeste fieri potest, ad veritatis iustitiaeque patrocinium
uti : elaborare, ut constitutum naturae Deique lege modum libertas
agendi ne transiliat : dare operam ut ad eam, quam diximus,
christianam similitudinem et formam omnis respublica traducatur.
—Harum rerum adipiscendarum ratio constitui uno certoque
modo haud commode potest, cum debeat singulis locis temporibus-
que, quae sunt multum inter se disparia, convenire. Nihilominus
conservanda in primis est voluntatum concordia, quaerendaque
agendorum similitudo. Atque optime utrumque impetrabitur, si
praescripta Sedis Apostolicae legem vitae singuli putent, atque
Episcopis obtemperent, quos *Spiritus sanctus posuit regere Ecclesiam
Dei.*[1]—Defensio quidem catholici nominis necessario postulat ut
in profitendis doctrinis, quae ab Ecclesia traduntur, una sit omnium
sententia, et summa constantia, et hac ex parte cavendum ne
quis opinionibus falsis aut ullo modo conniveat, aut mollius resis-
tat, quam veritas patiatur. De iis quae sunt opinabilia, licebit
cum moderatione studioque indagandae veritatis disputare, procul
tamen suspicionibus iniuriosis, criminationibusque mutuis.—Quam
ad rem, ne animorum coniunctio criminandi temeritate dirimatur,
sic intelligant universi : integritatem professionis catholicae consistere nequaquam posse cum opinionibus ad *naturalismum* vel
rationalismum accedentibus, quarum summa est tollere funditus
instituta christiana, hominisque stabilire in societate principatum,
posthabito Deo.—Pariter non licere aliam officii formam privatim
sequi, aliam publice, ita scilicet ut Ecclesiae auctoritas in vita
privata observetur, in publica respuatur. Hoc enim esset honesta
et turpia coniungere, hominemque secum facere digladiantem,
cum contra debeat sibi semper constare, neque ulla in re ullove
in genere vitae a virtute christiana deficere.—Verum si quaeratur
de rationibus mere politicis, de optimo genere reipublicae, de
ordinandis alia vel alia ratione civitatibus, utique de his rebus
potest honesta esse dissensio. Quorum igitur cognita ceteroqui
pietas est, animusque decreta Sedis Apostolicae obedienter acci-
pere paratus, iis vitio verti dissentaneam de rebus, quas diximus,
sententiam, iustitia non patitur : multoque est maior iniuria, si
in crimen violatae suspectaeve fidei catholicae, quod non semel
factum dolemus, adducantur.—Omninoque istud praeceptum

[1] Act. xx. 28.

teneant qui cogitationes suas solent mandare litteris, maximeque ephemeridum auctores. In hac quidem de rebus maximis contentione nihil est intestinis concertationibus, vel partium studiis relinquendum loci, sed conspirantibus animis studiisque id debent universi contendere, quod est commune omnium propositum, religionem remque publicam conservare. Si quid igitur dissidiorum antea fuit, oportet voluntaria quadam oblivione conterere: si quid temere, si quid iniuria actum, ad quoscumque demum ea culpa pertineat, compensandum est caritate mutua, et praecipuo quodam omnium in Apostolicam Sedem obsequio redimendum.—Hac via duas res praeclarissimas catholici consecuturi sunt, alteram, ut adiutores sese impertiant Ecclesiae in conservanda propagandaque sapientia christiana : alteram ut beneficio maximo afficiant societatem civilem, cuius, malarum doctrinarum cupiditatumque caussa, magnopere periclitatur salus.

Haec quidem, Venerabiles Fratres, habuimus, quae universis catholici orbis gentibus traderemus de civitatum constitutione christiana, officiisque civium singulorum.

Ceterum implorare summis precibus oportet caeleste praesidium, orandusque Deus, ut haec, quae ad ipsius gloriam communemque humani generis salutem cupimus et conamur, optatos ad exitus idem Ipse perducat, cuius est illustrare hominum mentes, permovere voluntates. Divinorum autem beneficiorum auspicem, et paternae benevolentiae Nostrae testem vobis, Venerabiles Fratres, et Clero populoque universo vestrae fidei vigilantiaeque commisso Apostolicam Benedictionem peramanter in Domino impertimus.

Datum Romae apud S. Petrum die i. Nov. an. MDCCCLXXXV. Pontificatus Nostri Anno octavo.

LEO PP. XIII.

TRANSLATION.

POPE LEO XIII.

VENERABLE BRETHREN,

HEALTH AND APOSTOLIC BENEDICTION.

THE CHURCH, the immortal work of the God of mercy, though she looks directly and essentially to the salvation of souls and to their obtaining the happiness of heaven, is even in temporal matters the source of benefits as many and as great as if she had been established chiefly and above all to insure the prosperity of this life on earth.—Wherever, indeed, the Church has set her foot, she has forthwith changed the face of things, and has imbued the manners of the people with a new civilisation and with virtues which were before unknown; and the nations that have received her have been distinguished by their gentleness and justice, and by the glory of their deeds.—But it is an old reproach, brought against the Church from early times, that she is out of harmony with the aspirations of society, and incapable of contributing in any way to the prosperity and refinement which are rightly and naturally sought for by every well-constituted State. We know that from the very beginning of the Church the Christians were harassed by evil opinions of this kind, and were held up to hatred and detestation for being, as they were called, enemies of the Empire: and Christianity was charged by the populace of those days with being the cause of the calamities that assailed the State, whereas, in reality, an avenging God was exacting just punishment from the guilty. This odious calumny, not without reason, armed the genius and sharpened the pen of St. Augustine, who, especially in his treatise *On the City of God,* set forth in so bright a light the value of Christian wisdom in its connection with the public weal, that he seems, not only to have pleaded the cause of the Christians of his day, but to have refuted these false charges for ever.—Yet the evil propensity to make such charges and accusations has not been set at rest. Many indeed have tried to elaborate a theory of civil society based on other doctrines than those approved of by the Catholic Church; and now, in these latter times, a novel jurisprudence has begun everywhere to grow up and to prevail, and is said to be the outcome of an age now fully developed, the offspring of a progressive liberty.—But, though many attempts have been made, it is clear that no better method has been found of establishing and ruling the State than that which is the result of the teaching of the Gospel.—We deem it, therefore, of the greatest moment, and a duty of Our apostolic office, to compare with Christian doctrine the new opinions advanced concerning the State; and by this means We trust that, as the truth shines forth, the causes of error and doubt will be removed, so that all may learn the supreme rules of life which they ought to follow and obey.

It is no difficult matter to determine what would be the form and character of the State if it were governed according to the principles of Christian philosophy.—Man's natural instinct is to live in civil society: for he cannot attain in solitude the necessary means of life, nor the development of his mental and moral faculties; and therefore, by a Divine provision, he is born for a domestic and civil union and association with men, by which alone the needs of life can be adequately supplied. But as no society can hold together unless some one be over all, directing all by the same efficacious impulse to a common object, every civilised community stands in need of a ruling authority; and this authority, no less than society itself, originates in nature, and therefore has for its author God Himself.—From this it follows that there can be no public power except from God. For God alone is the true and supreme Lord of the world; all things whatsoever must be subject to Him and must serve Him; so that whoever possess the right of governing have it from no other source than from God, the supreme Ruler of all. "There is no power but from God."[1]—The right of ruling, however, is not necessarily joined with any special form of government: it may assume either one

[1] Rom. xiii. 1.

form or another, provided that it be such as to insure the general welfare. But whatever be the form of government, rulers must be mindful of God, the supreme Ruler of the world, and must set Him before themselves as an example and a law in their administration. For as, in things that are visible, God has produced secondary causes, wherein the Divine nature and action can in some way be perceived, and which conduce to the end to which the course of the world is directed; so in civil society He has willed that there should be a ruling authority, and that they who hold it should be, as it were, an image of the Divine power and providence over mankind. The rule, therefore, must be just; and not that of a master, but like that of a father; for the power of God over man is most just and joined with a paternal goodness: and it must be carried on for the good of the citizens, because those who rule over others have authority only for the welfare of the State. Moreover the civil authority must not be subservient to the advantage of one or of a few, for it was established for the common good of all. But if those who are in authority rule unjustly; if they err through arrogance or pride; if their measures be injurious to the people; let them know that hereafter an account must be rendered to God, and the stricter in proportion to the sacredness of their office or the greatness of their dignity. "The mighty shall be mightily tormented."[1] —Thus, indeed, will the majesty of the law meet with honourable and willing reverence from the people; for when once they are convinced that rulers hold authority from God, they will feel that it is a matter of justice and duty to be obedient to them, and to show to them respect and fidelity with somewhat of the affection of children for their parents. "Let every soul be subject to higher powers."[2]—Indeed to contemn lawful authority, in whomsoever vested, is as unlawful as to resist the Divine will; and whoever resists that, rushes wilfully to destruction. "He that resisteth the power, resisteth the ordinance of God; and they that resist purchase to themselves damnation."[3] Wherefore to cast aside obedience, and by popular violence to incite the country to sedition, is treason, not only against man, but against God.

The State, being thus constituted, is clearly bound to satisfy its many and great duties towards God by the public profession of religion. Nature and reason which bind every individual reli-

[1] Wisd. vi. 7.   [2] Rom. xiii. 1.   [3] Rom. viii. 2.

giously to worship God, because we belong to Him, and must
return to Him from Whom we came, bind the civil community by
the same law. For men living together in society are no less
under the power of God than individuals are; and society,
no less than individuals, owes gratitude to God, its author, its
preserver, and the beneficent source of the innumerable blessings
which it has received. Therefore, as no one may neglect his
duties towards God; and as it is the first duty of every one to
embrace religion both in mind and heart—not such a religion as
each may choose, but that one which God commands, and which
by certain and undoubted marks is proved to be the only true
one; in like manner States cannot without crime act as though
God did not exist, or cast off the care of religion as alien to them
or useless, or out of several kinds of religion adopt whichever
they please; but they are absolutely bound to the worship of
God in the way that He has shown to be His will.—Therefore
among rulers the Name of God must be holy; and one of their
first duties must be to favour religion, to protect it, to cover it
with the authority of the laws, and not to institute or decree anything incompatible with its security. They owe this also to the
people over whom they rule. For we are all by birth and adop-
tion destined to enjoy, after this frail and short life, a supreme
and final good in heaven; and to this end all effort should be
referred. And because upon this depends the full and perfect
happiness of men, therefore the attainment of this end is of all
conceivable interests the most important. Hence civil society,
which has been established for the common welfare, must, while
guarding the prosperity of the community, so look to the interests
of its individual members as not to impede in any way, but to
facilitate as far as possible, the attainment of that supreme and
unchangeable good which they look for. For this, attention must
especially be paid to the most careful and inviolate preservation
of religion, by the practice of which man is united to God.

Which is the true religion it is not difficult for a man to dis-
cern, if only he will view the matter with a careful and unbiassed
judgment : for there are proofs of great number and splendour—
for example, the fulfilment of prophecies, numerous miracles, the
rapid spread of the faith in the midst of enemies and of the
greatest hindrances, the testimony of the martyrs, and the like;
by which it is evident that the only true religion is that which

Jesus Christ Himself instituted, and which He intrusted to His Church to defend and propagate.

For the only-begotten Son of God established a society on earth which is called the Church; and to it He transmitted the most high and divine office which He had received from His Father, to be perpetuated for ever. "As the Father hath sent Me, I also send you."[1] "Behold, I am with you all days, even to the consummation of the world."[2]—Therefore, as Jesus Christ came into the world that men might "have life, and have it more abundantly,"[3] so also the Church has for its aim and end the eternal salvation of souls: and for this cause it is so constituted as to embrace all mankind, without limit or circumscription of time or place. "Preach ye the Gospel to every creature."[4]—Over this immense multitude of men God Himself has set rulers with power to govern them; and He has willed that one should be head of all, and the chief and unerring teacher of truth, to whom He has given the keys of the kingdom of heaven. "To thee will I give the keys of the kingdom of heaven."[5] "Feed My lambs, feed My sheep."[6] "I have prayed for thee that thy faith fail not."[7]—This society, though it is composed of men just as civil society is, yet because of the end that it has in view, and the means by which it tends to it, is supernatural and spiritual; and, therefore, it is distinguished from civil society and differs from it; and, what is of the highest moment, it is a society juridically perfect in its kind, possessing in and by itself, by the will and beneficence of its Founder, all the appliances that are necessary for its preservation and action. Just as the end at which the Church aims is by far the noblest of ends, so its power is the most exalted of all powers, and cannot be regarded as inferior to the civil power or in any way subject to it.—In truth, Jesus Christ gave to His Apostles full authority as to sacred things; with the power of making laws properly so called; and the twofold right of judging and of punishing, which follows from it: "All power is given to Me in heaven and in earth; going therefore teach all nations .... teaching them to observe whatsoever I have commanded you."[8] And in another place: "If he will not hear them, tell the Church."[9] And again: "In readiness to revenge all

---

[1] John xx. 21.   [2] Matt. xxviii. 20.   [3] John x. 10.
[4] Mark xvi. 15.   [5] Matt. xvi. 19.   [6] John xxi. 16, 17.
[7] Luke xxii. 32.   [8] Matt. xxviii. 18, 19, 20.   [9] Matt. xviii. 17.

disobedience." [1] And once more: "That .... I may not deal more severely, according to the power which the Lord has given Me unto edification, and not unto destruction." [2] So then it is not the State, but the Church, that is to be man's guide to heaven. It is to her that God has assigned the office of seeing to, and of legislating for, all that concerns religion; of teaching all nations; of extending the Christian faith as far as possible; and, in a word, of administering its affairs freely and without hindrance, according to her own judgment.—Now this authority, perfect in itself and plainly independent, which has long been opposed by a philosophy subservient to princes, the Church has never ceased to claim for herself and publicly to exercise. The Apostles themselves were the first to maintain it, when, being forbidden by the leaders of the Synagogue to preach the Gospel, they boldly answered, "We must obey God rather than men." [3] This same authority the holy Fathers of the Church have been careful to maintain by weighty arguments as occasion arose; and the Roman Pontiffs have never ceased to defend it with inflexible constancy.—Nay more, princes and rulers have themselves approved it both in theory and in practice; for in the making of compacts, in the transaction of business, in sending and receiving ambassadors, and in the interchange of other good offices, it has been their custom to treat with the Church as with a supreme and legitimate power.—And, certainly, we must hold that it was not without a singular disposition of God's providence that this power of the Church was furnished with a civil sovereignty, as the surest safeguard of its independence.

God, therefore, has divided the charge of the human race between two powers, the ecclesiastical and the civil, the one being set over divine and the other over human things. Each is supreme in its kind: each has fixed limits within which it is contained, and those limits are defined by the nature and special object of each; so that there is, as it were, a circle marked out, within which each acts by its own right. But, inasmuch as each has authority over the same subjects, and it might come to pass that one and the same thing, though in different respects, yet still the same thing, might pertain to the jurisdiction and judgment of both, therefore God, Who foreseeth all things and Who

[1] 2 Cor. x. 6.　　　[2] 2 Cor. xiii. 10.　　　[3] Acts v. 29.

has established these two powers, has in due order arranged the
course of each in right relation to the other. "For the powers
that are, are ordained of God."[1] If it were not so, contentions
and conflicts would often arise ; and not unfrequently man would
hesitate in anxiety and doubt, like a traveller with two roads
before him, not knowing what course to follow ; with two powers
commanding contrary things, which he could not disobey without
neglect of duty. But it would be most repugnant to think this
of the wisdom and goodness of God ; for even in physical things,
though they are of a far lower order, He has so combined the
forces and causes of nature with a sort of wonderful harmony, that
none of them is a hindrance to the rest, and all of them most
fitly and aptly work together for the great end of the universe.—
There must, therefore, between these two powers be a certain
orderly connection, which may be compared to the union of the
soul and body in man. The nature and extent of that connection can be determined only, as We have said, by having regard
to the nature of each power, and taking account of the relative
excellence and nobility of their purpose ; for one of them has for
its proximate and chief object the comforts of this mortal life, the
other the everlasting joys of heaven.—Whatever, therefore, in
human things is in any way sacred; whatever pertains to the
salvation of souls or to the worship of God, either in its own
nature, or by reason of the end to which it is referred ; all this is
subject to the power and judgment of the Church : but all other
things, contained in the civil and political order, are rightly subject to the civil authority; for Jesus Christ has commanded that
what is Cæsar's shall be rendered to Cæsar, and what belongs to
God shall be rendered to God.—There are times, however, when
another method of concord is available for peace and liberty ; We
mean when rulers and the Roman Pontiff come to an understanding concerning any particular matter. At such times the Church
gives singular proof of her maternal love, by the greatest possible
kindness and indulgence.

Such then, as We have briefly indicated, is the Christian organi-
sation of civil society: no rash or fanciful fiction, but deduced
from the highest and truest principles, which are confirmed by
natural reason itself.

In such a conformation of the State there is nothing that can

[1] Rom. xiii. 1.

be thought unworthy of the dignity of rulers, or unbecoming; and so far is it from lessening the rights of sovereignty, that it adds to it stability and grandeur. For, if it be fully considered, this conformation has a great perfection, which all others lack; and from it various excellent results would follow, if each part would keep its place and discharge fully the office and work to which it is appointed.—In truth, in the constitution of the State such as We have described, Divine and human things are properly divided; the rights of citizens are assured, and defended by Divine, natural, and human law; and the duties of every one are wisely marked out, and their fulfilment is well insured. In their uncertain and laborious journey to the everlasting city, all men see that they have safe guides and helpers on their way; and they know also that they have others whose business it is to protect them and their property, and to obtain or secure for them all other things that are essential for this life.—Domestic society acquires that firmness and solidity which it needs, in the sanctity of marriage one and indissoluble; the rights and duties of husband and wife are regulated with wise justice and equity; due honour is secured to the woman; the authority of the man is conformed to the example of the authority of God; the power of the father is tempered by a due regard for the dignity of the wife and off-spring; and the best possible provision is made for the guardianship, for the welfare, and for the education of the children.—In the political and civil affairs the laws aim at the common good, and are not determined by the deceptive wishes and judgments of the multitude, but by truth and justice; the authority of rulers is vested with a sacredness more than human, and is restrained from deviating from justice and overstepping the limits of power; and the obedience of citizens is rendered with honour and dignity, because it is not the servitude of man to man, but obedience to the will of God exercising His sovereignty by means of men. And this being recognised and admitted, it is felt to be just that the dignity of rulers should be respected, that the public authority should be constantly and faithfully obeyed, that no act of sedition should be committed, and that the civil order of the State should be kept intact.—So also, in the duties of one to another, there are charity, kindness, and liberality; the man who is at once a citizen and a Christian is not distracted by conflicting obligations; and, lastly, the abundant benefits with which the

Christian religion of its own accord enriches even the mortal life of man, are acquired for the community and civil society, so that it may be said with the fullest truth : " The state of the commonwealth depends on the religion with which God is worshipped, and between the one and the other there is a close relation and connection."—Admirably, as he is accustomed, does St. Augustine in many places dilate on the force of these advantages, but especially when he addresses the Catholic Church in these words : " Thou trainest and instructest children with tenderness, young men with vigour, old men with gentleness, according as the age, not of the body only, but of the mind of each requires. Women thou subjectest to their husbands in chaste and faithful obedience, not for the satisfaction of lust, but for the propagation of offspring, and participation in the affairs of the family. Thou settest husbands over their wives, not that they may trifle with the weaker sex, but in accordance with the laws of true affection. Thou subjectest children to their parents in a kind of free service, and settest parents over their children with a benignant rule. . . . . Thou joinest together, not merely in society, but in a kind of fraternity, citizens with citizens, nations with nations, and the whole race of men, by reminding them of their common parentage. Thou teachest kings to look to the interests of their people ; thou admonishest the people to submit to their kings. With all care thou teachest to whom honour is due, and affection, and reverence, and fear, and consolation, and admonition, and exhortation, and discipline, and reproach, and punishment; showing how all of these are not equally suitable to all, but that charity is due to all, and wrong to none."—And, in another place, reprehending the false wisdom of certain political philosophers, he observes : " Let those who say that the doctrine of Christ is hurtful to the State produce an army of soldiers such as the doctrine of Christ has commanded them to be; such governors of provinces, such husbands and wives, such parents and children, such masters and servants, such kings, such judges, and such payers and collectors of taxes, as the Christian teaching would have them to be ; and then let them dare to say that such teaching is hurtful to the State. Nay, rather they will not hesitate to confess that this teaching, if duly practised, is of great safety to the State."

There was once a time when States were governed by their

philosophy of the Gospel; when the power and divine virtue of Christian wisdom had penetrated into the laws, institutions, and manners of nations, and into all ranks and relations of civil society; when the religion instituted by Jesus Christ, established firmly in becoming dignity, flourished everywhere, by the favour of rulers and the due protection of magistrates; when Church and State were happily united in concord and friendly interchange of offices. The State thus composed brought forth fruits above all expectation, the memory of which still flourishes and will flourish, attested by innumerable monuments which can be neither destroyed nor obscured by any art of the adversary.— If Christian Europe subdued barbarous nations, and transferred them from a savage to a civilised state, from superstition to the truth; if she victoriously repelled the invasions of the Mahometans; if she has herself retained the primacy of civilisation, and become the leader and instructor of others in everything that adorns humanity; if she has granted to the nations a true and manifold liberty; if she has most wisely established numerous institutions for the solace of human misery; beyond all controversy this is due in great measure to religion, under whose auspices these great undertakings were commenced, and with whose aid they were accomplished. The same excellent state of things would, indeed, have continued if the agreement of the two powers had lasted; and greater things might well have been expected, if there had been obedience to the authority, the teaching, and the counsels of the Church, characterised by greater faithfulness and perseverance. For that is to be regarded as a perpetual law which Ivo of Chartres wrote to Pope Paschal II. : "When the kingdom and the priesthood are agreed between themselves, the world is well ruled, and the Church flourishes and bears fruit. But when they are at variance, not only small things do not increase, but even great things fall into miserable decay."

But that fatal and deplorable passion for innovation which was aroused in the sixteenth century, first threw the Christian religion into confusion, and then, by natural sequence, passed on to philosophy, and thence pervaded all ranks of society. From this source, as it were, issued those later maxims of unbridled liberty which, in the midst of the terrible disturbances of the last century, were excogitated and proclaimed as the principles and foundation of that new jurisprudence, previously unknown, which, in many points, is out of harmony, not only with the Christian law, but with the natural law also.--Amongst these principles the chief one is that which proclaims that all men, as by race and nature they are alike, are also equal in their life; that each is so far master of himself as in no way to come under the authority of another; that he is free to think on every subject as he likes, and to act as he pleases; that no man has any right to rule over others. In a society founded upon these principles, government is only the will of the people, which, as it is under the power of itself alone, so is alone its own ruler. It chooses, nevertheless, those to whom it shall intrust itself; but in such a way that it transfers to them, not so much the right, as the office of governing, which is to be exercised in its name. The authority of God is passed over in silence, as if either there were no God, or He cared nothing for human society; as if men, either as individuals or in society, owed nothing to God; or as if there could be a government of which the whole cause, and power, and authority, do not reside in God Himself. In this way, as is evident, a State becomes nothing but a multitude, mistress and governor of itself. And since the people is said to contain in itself the source of all rights and of all power, it follows that the State does not deem itself bound by any kind of duty towards God; that it makes no public profession of religion; that it does not hold itself bound to inquire which of the many religions is the only true one, nor to prefer one religion to the rest, and to show it special favour; but rather to give equal rights to all religions, to the end that the public order shall not incur injury from any of them. It is a part of this theory that all questions concerning religion are to be referred to private judgment; that every one is allowed to follow whichever religion he prefers, or none at all if he approves of none. Hence these consequences naturally arise: the judgment of each conscience is without regard to law; the freest opinions are expressed as to the practice or neglect of Divine worship; and there is unbounded license for men to think what they like, and to publish what they think.

Such foundations of the State being laid, which at this time are in general favour, it easily appears into what an unjust position the Church is driven.—When the conduct of affairs is in accordance with doctrines of this kind, to the Catholic religion is assigned only a position equal or inferior to that of alien societies; no regard is paid to ecclesiastical laws; and the Church, which, by the command and mandate of Jesus Christ, ought to teach all nations, finds herself forbidden in any way to deal with the public instruction of the people.—As for matters which are of mixed jurisdiction, the rulers of the civil power lay down the law at their own pleasure, and in this matter haughtily set aside the most sacred laws of the Church. Wherefore they bring under their own jurisdiction the marriages of Christians, deciding even as to the marriage bond, and as to the unity and indissolubility of marriage. They lay their hands on the goods of the clergy, denying that the Church can hold property. Finally, they so act with regard to the Church that, rejecting altogether her claim to the nature and rights of a perfect society, they hold her to be in no way different from other societies in the State; and on that account, if she possesses any right or legal means of acting, she is said to hold it by the concession and favour of the government.—If in any State the Church, with the approval of the civil laws, retains her own right, and an agreement has been publicly made between the two powers, men begin to cry out that the affairs of the Church must be severed from those of the State, wishing thereby to violate with impunity their pledged faith, and to have unchecked control over all things.—And as the Church, unable to desert her greatest and most sacred duties, cannot endure this patiently, and asks that the pledge given to her be fully and religiously kept, contests frequently arise between the sacred and the civil power, of which the result commonly is that the weaker yields to the one which is stronger in human resources.

So it is the custom and the wish in this condition of public affairs, which is now admired by many, either to expel the Church altogether, or to keep it under restraint and in bondage to the State. Public Acts, in great measure, are framed with this design. Laws, public administration, education without religion, the spoliation and destruction of Religious Orders, the overturning of the civil sovereignty of the Roman Pontiffs, all look to this one end—to enervate Christian institutions, to narrow the liberty of the Catholic Church, and to destroy her other rights.

Natural reason itself convinces us that such opinions as to the government of a State are at variance with the truth.—Nature bears witness that all power, of whatever kind, emanates from God, as from its chief and most august source. The doctrine that popular sovereignty, irrespective of God, resides in the masses, is indeed a doctrine exceedingly well calculated to flatter, and to inflame many passions; but it lacks all rational proof, and has not the power of insuring public safety and the maintenance of order. Indeed, from the prevalence of this teaching, things have come to such a pass that many regard it as a law of civil jurisprudence that seditions may be rightly enkindled. For the opinion prevails that princes are nothing more than delegates appointed to carry out the will of the people; and therefore that all things are in like manner changeable at the popular will, so that the fear of public disturbance is for ever hanging over our heads.

As regards religion, to hold that there is no difference between forms that are unlike and contrary to each other, must clearly lead in the end to the rejection of all religion, both in theory and in practice. And this, if indeed it differs from atheism in name, is in fact the same thing. Men who really believe in the existence of God, if they are to be consistent and to avoid absurdity, must of necessity understand that different methods of divine worship, involving dissimilarity and conflict even on the most important points, cannot be all equally probable, equally good, and equally acceptable to God.

So also the freedom of thinking and of writing whatever one likes, without restraint, is not of itself an advantage at which society may rightly rejoice, but, on the contrary, a source and origin of many evils.—Liberty, inasmuch as it is a virtue perfecting man, should have truth and goodness for its object. But goodness and truth cannot be changed at man's pleasure ; they remain ever the same, and are not less unchangeable than Nature herself. If the mind assents to false opinions, and the will chooses what is evil and follows it, neither will attain to perfection, but both will fall from their natural dignity and will become corrupt. Whatever things, therefore, are contrary to virtue and truth, such things it is not right to put glaringly before the eyes of men; still less to defend them by the favour and protection of the law. A well-spent life is the only way to heaven, to which we all tend; and on this account the State departs from the laws and dictates of nature if it allows the license of opinion and of action to lead minds astray from the truth, and souls from the practice of virtue.—To exclude the Church, which God Himself has constituted, from the business of life, from the laws, from the teaching of youth, from domestic society, is a great and fatal error. A State from which religion is banished can never be well-regulated; and already, perhaps, more than need be is known of the nature and tendency of that *civil* philosophy of life and morals, as it is called. The Church of Christ is the true teacher of virtue and guardian of morals; she it is that protects the principles from which duties are derived, and, by proposing most efficacious reasons for a virtuous life, bids us not only to fly from wicked deeds, but to curb also the motions of the mind which are contrary to reason, even though no act should follow from them.—To wish the Church in the discharge of her duty to be subject to the civil power, is a great rashness and a great injustice. If this is done, order is disturbed, as things natural are thus put before things which are above nature; the many benefits which the Church, if free to act, would confer on society are either prevented, or at least diminished in number; and the way is prepared for enmities and conflicts between the two powers, with an evil result to both of which we have a too frequent experience.

Such doctrines as these, which are not approved by human reason, and are of the greatest gravity as regards civil discipline, the Roman Pontiffs Our predecessors, well understanding what the apostolic office required of them, by no means allowed to go forth without condemnation. Thus Gregory XVI., by the Encyclical Letter *Mirari vos*, of August 15th, 1832, inveighed with weighty words against these doctrines which were already being preached: namely, that no choice ought to be made of any particular form of worship; that it is right for individuals to judge of religion according to their personal preferences; that each man's conscience is to himself his sole sufficient guide; and that it is lawful for every man to promulgate whatsoever he may think, and to conspire against the State. On the question of the separation of Church and State, the same Pontiff speaks thus: "Nor can we hope for happier results, either for religion or for the civil government, from the wishes of those who desire that

the Church be separated from the State, and the agreement
between the secular power and the sacerdotal authority be broken
up. It is evident that these lovers of a shameless liberty are in
dread of an agreement which has always been of good augury,
and advantageous both to sacred and civil interests."—To the
like effect Pius IX., when opportunity offered, noted many false
opinions which had begun to prevail, and subsequently ordered
them to be collected together, in order that in this great conflux
of error Catholics might have something which they could safely
follow.[1]

From these decisions of the Popes it is clearly to be understood that the origin of public power is to be sought for in God
Himself, and not in the multitude; that free play for sedition is
repugnant to reason; that it is unlawful for the State, as it is for
the individual, either to disregard all religious duties, or to make
equal account of different kinds of religion; that the uncontrolled
liberty of thinking and publicly proclaiming one's thoughts is not
inherent in the rights of citizens, and is not on any account to be
reckoned worthy of favour or patronage.—In like manner it is
to be understood that the Church, no less than the State itself, is
a society perfect in its nature and in its right; and that those
who exercise sovereignty ought not so to act as to compel the
Church to become subservient or subject to them, or to restrict
her liberty in managing her own affairs, or to take away
aught from the other rights which have been conferred upon her
by Jesus Christ.—In matters, however, of mixed jurisdiction, it is
in the highest degree in accordance with nature and also with
the designs of God—not that one power should secede from the
other, still less that they should come into conflict, but that such

[1] It will suffice to indicate a few of them:

Prop. xix. The Church is not a true, perfect, and wholly independent society,
possessing its own unchanging rights conferred upon it by its Divine Founder;
but it is for the civil power to determine what are the rights of the Church, and
the limits within which it may use them.

Prop. xxxix. The State, as the origin and source of all rights, has a right
that is unlimited.

Prop. lv. The Church must be separated from the State, and the State from
the Church.

Prop. lxxix. . . . It is untrue that the civil liberty of every form of worship,
and the full power given to all of openly and publicly manifesting whatsoever
opinions and thoughts, lead to the more easy corruption of the minds and morals
of the people, and to the spread of the plague of religious indifference.

concord should be preserved between them as is suited to the
end for which each power exists.

Such, then, is the teaching of the Catholic Church concerning
the constitution and government of the State.—By these words
and decrees, if the matter be judged dispassionately, none of
the various forms of government is in itself condemned, inasmuch
as they have nothing repugnant to Catholic doctrine, and are
able, if wisely and justly managed, to insure the welfare of the
State.—Neither is it at all reprehensible in itself for the people
to have a greater or less share in the government; for at certain
times, and under certain laws, such participation may not only be
of benefit to the citizens, but even be their duty.—Nor is there
any reason why any one should accuse the Church of being want-
ing in gentleness, or opposed to real and legitimate liberty.—
The Church, it is true, deems it unlawful to place the various
forms of Divine worship on the same footing as the true religion;
still it does not on that account condemn those rulers who, for
the sake of securing some great good or preventing some great
evil, allow by custom and usage each kind of religion to have its
place in the State.—Indeed, the Church is wont diligently to take
care that no one shall be compelled against his will to embrace
the Catholic Faith; for, as St. Augustine wisely reminds us,
" Man cannot believe otherwise than of his own free will."

In like manner the Church cannot approve of that liberty which
begets a contempt of the most sacred laws of God, and casts off
the obedience due to lawful authority. For this is license rather
than liberty, and is most correctly called by St. Augustine, " the
liberty of perdition;" and by the Apostle St. Peter, "a cloak for
malice."[1]   Indeed, since it is contrary to reason, it is a true
servitude; "for whosoever committeth sin is the servant of sin."[2]
On the other hand, that liberty is real and to be sought after
which, in regard to the individual, allows not men to be the
slaves of error and of passion, the worst of masters; which, in
public administration, wisely directs the citizens, and provides
them with increased means of welfare; and which protects the
State from foreign interference.—This honest liberty, worthy of
man, the Church approves above all, and has never ceased in her
endeavour to keep it firm and undiminished among the people.
—In truth, whatever in the State is of chief avail for the common

[1] 1 Peter ii. 16.   [2] John viii. 34.

safety ; whatever has been usefully instituted to curb the license of rulers when opposed to the interests of the people, or to restrain the central authority from unwarrantable interference in municipal or family affairs ; whatever tends to preserve in individual citizens their honour, and manhood, and equal rights,—of all these things, as the monuments of past ages bear witness, the Catholic Church has always been either the author, the promoter, or the guardian. Ever therefore consistent with herself, while, on the one hand, she rejects that immoderate liberty which, in individuals and in nations, ends in license or servitude ; on the other, she willingly and with pleasure accepts whatever improvements the age brings forth, if they really secure the prosperity of this life, which is as it were a stage in the journey to the life which will be everlasting.—Therefore, when men say that the Church is jealous of modern political systems, and that she repudiates all the discoveries of modern thought, they utter a vain and groundless calumny. Wild opinions she repudiates, and condemns wicked projects of sedition, and that habit of mind which is the beginning of a voluntary departure from God ; but, as all truth must necessarily proceed from God, in whatever truth is attained by research the Church sees, as it were, a vestige of the Divine intelligence. And, as there is in nature no truth that can destroy belief in the doctrines of revelation, but much that will confirm it ; and as every newly-discovered truth may serve to further the knowledge or praise of God Himself ; therefore whatever extends the range of knowledge will always be willingly and joyfully accepted by the Church ; and, as she does in other branches of knowledge, she will encourage and promote those also which are concerned with the investigation of nature. In these studies, if the mind finds anything new the Church is not opposed to it ; she objects not to search being made for things that minister to the adornments and comforts of life : on the contrary, opposed as she always is to inertness and sloth, she earnestly wishes that the talents of men may, by cultivation and exercise, bear rich fruit ; she gives encouragement to every kind of art and handicraft ; and directing by her influence all these efforts to virtue and salvation, she strives to prevent man's intelligence and industry turning him away from God and from heavenly things.

All this, though so reasonable and full of forethought, finds little favour at this time, when States not only refuse to conform to the laws of Christian wisdom, but seem even to wish to depart each day farther from them.—Nevertheless, as truth brought to light is wont of its own accord to spread widely, and by degrees to pervade the minds of men, We, therefore, moved by the great and holy duty of Our Apostolic mission to all nations, speak freely as We ought: not that our eyes are closed to the spirit of the times, or that We repudiate the honest and useful improvements of our age; but because We wish the affairs of State to take a safer course than they do, and to rest on a more firm foundation, without detriment to the true freedom of the people; for the best parent and guardian of liberty amongst men is truth: " The truth shall make you free." [1]

If, in this difficult course of events, Catholics, as it behoves them, will listen to Us, they will easily see what are the duties of each one, in matters of *opinion* as well as in *action*.—As regards *opinion*, whatever the Roman Pontiffs have taught, or shall hereafter teach, must be held with a firm grasp of mind, and, as often as occasion requires, must be openly professed. Especially in regard to the *liberties*, so called, which are sought after in these days, all must stand by the judgment of the Apostolic See, and think as she does. Let no man be deceived by the good appearance of these things; but let him reflect whence they have begun, and by what efforts they are everywhere sustained and promoted. Experience has made us well acquainted with their results to the State; for everywhere they have borne fruits which good and wise men deplore.—If there exists anywhere, or if we imagine, a State wantonly and tyrannically waging war against Christianity, and we compare with it that modern form of government which We have described, the latter may seem the more tolerable of the two; still, the principles on which it is grounded are undoubtedly, as We have said, such as, in themselves, no man can approve.

Action may relate to private and domestic affairs, or to affairs public.—As to private affairs, man's first duty is to conform his life and conduct to the precepts of the Gospel, and not to hold back if Christian virtue demands of him something that is difficult to bear. All, moreover, are bound to love the Church as their common mother; to obey her laws, promote her honour, and defend her rights; and to endeavour to make her respected

[1] John viii. 32.

and beloved by those over whom they have authority.—
It is also of great importance to the public welfare pru-
dently to take part in the administration of municipal affairs;
and, above all, to endeavour to pass effective measures, so
that, as becomes a Christian people, public provision may be
made for the instruction of the young in religion and true morality;
for upon these things depends much the welfare of every State.
—Besides, it is in general useful and right for Catholics to extend
their exertions beyond this narrower field, and to give attention
to national politics. We say in *general*, because these Our precepts are addressed to all nations; but it may somewhere happen
that, for most urgent and just reasons, it is by no means expedient
for Catholics to engage in public affairs, or to take an active part
in politics. Generally, however, as We have said, to take no part
in public affairs, would be as wrong as to bestow no care or
labour for the common good; and the more so because Catholics
are admonished by the very doctrines they profess to be upright
and faithful in the discharge of office: but if they remain inactive,
men whose opinions give but small guarantee for the well-being
of the State will easily seize the reins of government. This
would be injurious also to Christianity; because those would be
in power who are badly disposed towards the Church, and those
least powerful who are well disposed. Wherefore there is evi-
dently just cause why Catholics should take part in the conduct
of public affairs: for they do not assume these responsibilities
in approval of what is unlawful in the methods of government at
this time; but in order that they may turn these very methods,
as far as may be, to the real and true public good, and at the
same time use their best endeavours to infuse, as it were, into
all the veins of the State the healthy sap and blood of Catholic
wisdom and virtue.—So was it in the early ages of the Church.
The manners and aspirations of the heathens widely differed
from those of the Gospel; yet Christians were everywhere to be
seen undefiled in the midst of heathen superstition, and, while
always true to themselves, strenuously coming forward whenever
an opening was presented. Models of fidelity to their princes,
obedient, as far as was lawful, to the sovereign power, they
everywhere cast around them a halo of sanctity; they sought
the advantage of their brethren, and drew others to the wisdom
of Christ; yet were bravely prepared to retire from public life,

and even to die, if they could not retain honours, or magistracy, or command, without loss of virtue. For this reason Christian customs soon found their way, not only into private houses, but into the camp, the senate, and even the imperial palace. "We are but of yesterday," said Tertullian, "yet we crowd everything belonging to you: cities, islands, villages, towns, assemblies, the army itself; your wards and corporations, the palace, the senate, and the law courts." So that the Christian faith, when once it became lawful publicly to profess the Gospel, appeared in most of the cities of the Empire, not like a child crying in its cradle, but already grown up and strong.

In these days it is well to revive these examples of our fore-fathers.—First of all, it behoves all Catholics who are worthy of the name, to be, and to wish to be known as, most loving chil-dren of the Church; to reject without hesitation whatever is inconsistent with this fair name; to make use of popular insti-tutions, as far as can honestly be done, for the advantage of truth and justice; to see that liberty shall not transgress the bounds fixed by nature and the law of God; to endeavour to bring back all civil society to that likeness and form of Christianity which We have described.—It is hardly possible to lay down any one fixed method whereby these objects are to be attained; because the method must suit separate places and times, which differ greatly from one another. Nevertheless, before all things, unity of purpose must be preserved, and similarity must be sought for in the plans of action. Both these objects will be attained with-out fail, if all will regard the directions of the Apostolic See as their rule of life, and obey the Bishops whom "the Holy Ghost has placed to rule the Church of God."[1]—Indeed, the defence of Catholicity necessarily demands that, in the profession of doctrines taught by the Church, all shall be unanimous and constant; and care must be taken never to connive in any way at false opinions, or to resist them less strenuously than truth will allow. In mere matters of opinion, it is lawful to discuss things with moderation and with a desire of investigating the truth, without injurious suspicions or recrimination.—Wherefore, lest concord be broken by rash charges, let this be understood by all: that the integrity of Catholic faith is incompatible with opinions approaching either to *naturalism* or *rationalism;* the essence of which is utterly to

[1] Acts xx. 28.

do away with Christianity, and to establish the supremacy of man in society, to the exclusion of God.—That likewise it is unlawful to follow one line of duty in private and another in public, privately respecting the authority of the Church, and publicly rejecting it: for this would be to join together good and evil, and to put man in conflict with himself; whereas he ought always to be consistent, and never in the least thing or in any mode of life to decline from Christian virtue.—But in merely political matters, as to the best form of government, or different systems of administration, concerning these things a difference of opinion is lawful. Those, therefore, whose piety is in other respects known, and whose minds are ready to accept in all obedience the decrees of the Apostolic See, cannot in justice be accounted as bad men because they disagree on the subjects We have mentioned; and still graver wrong will be done to them, if, as We have more than once seen with regret, they are accused of violating, or of wavering in, the Catholic faith.—Let this be well borne in mind by all who are in the habit of committing their thoughts to writing, and above all by journalists. In the struggle for interests of the highest order there is no room for intestine strife or party rivalries; but all must endeavour with one mind and purpose to secure that which is the common object of all, the preservation of Religion and of the State. If, therefore, hitherto there have been dissensions, let them henceforth be cheerfully buried in oblivion. If rash or injurious actions have been done, whoever may have been in fault, let mutual charity make amends, and let the past be redeemed by a special obedience of all to the Apostolic See.— In this way Catholics will attain two most excellent objects: they will become helpers to the Church in preserving and propagating Christian wisdom; and they will confer the greatest benefit on civil society, the safety of which is exceedingly endangered by evil doctrines and passions.

This, Venerable Brethren, is what We have thought it Our duty to expound to all nations of the Catholic world regarding the Christian Constitution of States, and the duties of individual citizens.

We must now with most earnest prayer implore the protection of Heaven, beseeching God, Who alone can enlighten the minds of men and move their will, to bring to pass, for His glory and for the salvation of mankind, those things which We long for, and for which We strive. As a pledge of divine benefits, and in token of Our paternal benevolence, to you, Venerable Brethren, and to the Clergy and to the whole people committed to your care and vigilance, We lovingly grant in the Lord the Apostolic Benediction.

Given in Rome, at St. Peter's, on the first day of November, in the year MDCCCLXXXV., the eighth year of Our Pontificate.

POPE LEO XIII.

www.ingramcontent.com/pod-product-compliance
Lightning Source LLC
Chambersburg PA
CBHW021432090426

42739CB00009B/1454